INTRODUCTION
TO ACOUSTIC BLUES
BY KENNY SULTAN

I would like to thank **James Edwards** for his help with transcribing my sloppy tabulature into coherent music notation. James is a fine guitarist, and if you are interested in some of his recording, you can contact me at my address.

I would also like to thank **Karen Painter** for taking the rough draft of the book and making it look logical.

I cannot forget **Mark Mosrie** who supplied some of the photographs. He is always willing to help without asking for anything in return.

Cover photo -© Tone Anaderaa
Photo tinting – Eddie Young
Layout & Production – Ron Middlebrook

ISBN 978-1-70519-298-6
SAN 683-8022

Contents

CD Track List　　　　　　　　　　　　　　　　　　　　　**Page**

ABOUT THE AUTHOR

Kenny Sultan has been playing guitar since the age of seven. Soon thereafter, his brother introduced him to the blues of T-bone Walker and Lightnin' Hopkins. The effect was permanent.

A noted teacher, he has taught music, guitar and blues at the college level. He has also conducted workshops and seminars throughout the country.

He has four albums to his credit with his partner Tom Ball and has appeared as a sideman on numerous recordings by other artists.

He currently resides in Santa Barbara, CA.

Foreword

The purpose of this book is to present an primary introduction to acoustic blues guitar. You should already know the basic chords and have some prior experience playing the guitar. We will cover blues in five different keys and positions; A, C, D, E and G. These are the keys that I primarily use. (Besides, who in their right mind would ever want to play acoustic blues in D flat?) Each position will have its own unique sound, and with the use of a capo, learning these five positions (A, C, D, E, G) will allow you to play blues in any key. Along with the basic blues rhythms and leads, fingerstyle blues will be covered, using both an alternating and monotone bass. The "down home" style of guitar playing, similar to Lightnin' Hopkins, John Lee Hooker, Brownie McGhee and John Hammond will be touched upon, as well as the lighter and bouncier playing of Blind Blake, Rev. Gary Davis and Blind Boy Fuller. Near the end of the book, we will discuss open tuning and bottleneck guitar. On the cassette tape that accompanies this book I play each example and every song, most of the songs are played in slow speed and at regular tempo.

Blues guitar is different than other styles of guitar in that there is more feel involved than technique. It is very important that you use the tablature only as a guide to your ears. The accompanying tape will be your most valuable tool. All the nuances of the blues cannot be written down properly; listening is the only way to really absorb all the material. My suggestion is to listen to the tape before you try any of the songs. Hear exactly what you're supposed to do, then read the music to help you create the sound desired. In my workshops, classes and private lessons, I urge my students to learn everything by ear. I rarely use written music, but under these circumstances the written notation should be used, but not relied upon exclusively. Memorize each song, then put the written material away. Try to let your own personal feelings come through in your playing. Make each song a personal experience. Remember, this isn't classical music, so play it loose. Don't worry about mistakes, and above all, have fun.

-Basic 12-Bar Blues Progression-

It is important to understand the basic 12-bar blues progression before going on to more complicated material and learning songs. The three main chords utilized in the blues are the I, IV and V, also known as the tonic, sub-dominant and dominant chords.

The tonic chord (I) is taken from the first note of the scale.

The sub-dominant (IV) is taken from the fourth note of the scale

The dominant (V) from the fifth note.

Using this method, a basic 12-bar blues progression would look like this:

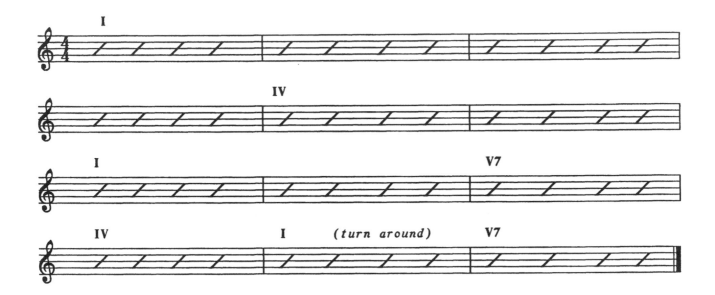

First of all, let's try to make music out of this mess. There are several ways to do this. I could list all of the chords in each key, but I'm not sure you're going to be able to take this book everywhere you go, or if you're at a blues jam session, that you would be able to remember all the chords... especially after a couple of beers. But just in case, here's the list:

Key of A: A, D, E

Key of B flat (A sharp): B flat (A sharp), E flat (D sharp), F

Key of B: B, E, F sharp (G flat)

Key of C: C, F, G

Key of D flat (C sharp): D flat (C sharp), G flat (F sharp) A flat (G sharp)

Key of D: D, G, A

Key of E flat (D sharp): E flat (D sharp), A flat (G sharp) B flat (A sharp)

Key of E: E, A, B

Key of F: F, B flat (A sharp), C

Key of F sharp (G flat): F sharp (G flat), B, C sharp (D flat)

Key of G: G, C, D

Key of A flat (G sharp): A flat (G sharp), D flat (C sharp), E flat (D sharp)

If you don't have the book with you, there are two other ways of finding out the chords. These might look very unorthodox, but trust me... they work. There are 5 basic keys that we will be playing blues with in this book: A, C, D, E and G. To help memorize these keys, think of the word "CAGED". If the song is in one of these keys, you can figure out the chords with the use of one of your hands.

Let's say you want to play 12-bar blues in the key of A. Using your right hand,
**count "A" on your thumb,
move up the alphabet to "B" on your index finger,
"C" on your middle finger,
"D" on your ring finger,
"E" on your pinkie.**

Your thumb will be the "I" chord, your index finger the "II" chord, your middle finger the "III" chord, your ring finger the "IV" chord and your pinkie the "V" chord. Again, count up the alphabet, ABCDE, from your thumb to your pinkie, and the chords that fall on your thumb, ring finger and pinkie will be the I, IV and V. Two words of caution: Anyone that sees you doing this will think you're nuts... and it only works with the I, IV and V chords; not with the II, III, IV or VII chords of any particular key.

As an example, let's say some friends of yours want to play blues in the key of C. You don't happen to know the chords of the key of C offhand, so behind your back (or your guitar) you count, C, D, E, F, G. "C" being the "I" chord, "F" the "IV" chord and "G" the "V" chord. Now, put these in the 12-bar blues form we've just covered, and you're ready to play.

What if you're not playing in one of these 5 keys? How do you find the proper chords? Use your guitar! If you know the notes on your guitar (I hope you do), it's easy to find the proper chords. I use my 6th string. First, find the tonic on the 6th string. For example, if you want to play in the key of F, find the "F" note on the 6th string (the 1st fret). To find the "IV" chord from the tonic, count 5 frets up the neck. Is it a B flat note? Count 7 frets up from the tonic to find the dominant "C" note. You can also find the dominant by counting 2 frets, or 1 step up, from the sub-dominant chord; B flat to C, 6th fret to 8th fret.

Try this with several different keys and refer back to the list of chords that were given to you earlier to make sure you are correct. I should let you know that to get the "bluesiest" sound possible, you should make the "V" chord a dominant 7th (B7, C7, D7, etc.), and most of the time, add a 7th note to the "IV" chord.

I think this has been enough on the technical side of the blues. The best way to learn is to just play it, so let's get to the music.

CHICAGO
BLUES
FESTIVAL

My favorite key for playing the blues is the key of E. The chords used in the key of E are: E, A and B7. Each chord has its own unique character. In addition to sounding great, the E and A chords have an open string for their tonic note; the open 6th string for the E chord and the open 5th string for the A chord. This is a definite plus, which we will discover later.

RHYTHM

Before going on to learn the more intricate aspects of blues guitar playing, it is necessary to develop a good, solid foundation of rhythm techniques. The most familiar rhythm lick in the key of E is called the shuffle. It looks like this:

Blues Shuffle in E

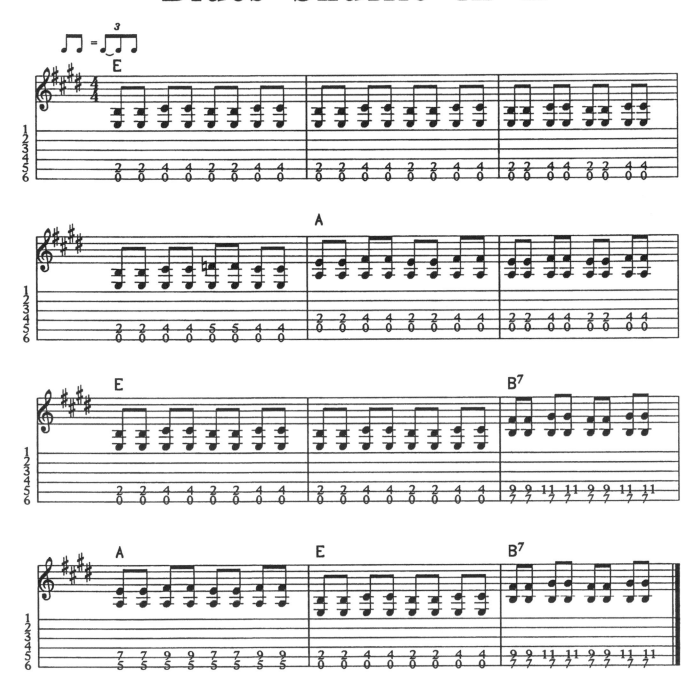

It is very important to listen to the accompanying tape to hear exactly how the rhythm should be played. Another good rhythm technique is the single string shuffle or single string boogie. The same shuffle rhythm should be used, but this time hit only one string at a time.

Single String Shuffle

Again, listen to the tape to hear what it should sound like.

Once you are comfortable with these exercises and have developed a feel for the proper rhythm of the shuffle, we can now move on and try to play rhythm and lead guitar at the same time. In this technique, the thumb of the right hand pounds out the rhythm while the 1st and 2nd fingers play the lead, or "fill". With the E chord, every time you tap your foot, hit the open 6th string. In other words, on every downbeat, hit the open E with the thumb of your right hand. Here's an example:

Example 1

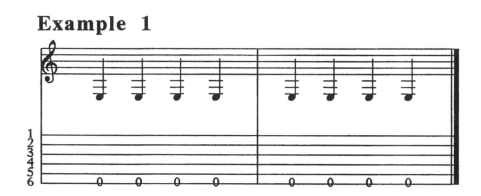

By adding the open 1st string, or high E, it would now look like this:

Example 2

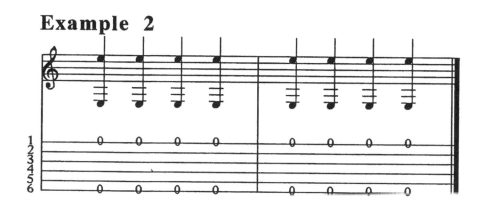

In the above example, the lead notes occur right on the beat. This is a **pinch** with your thumb and one of your fingers, preferably the index or middle. In the example below, the treble notes occur in between the beats. Count "one and two and three and four", placing the first string notes on the upbeat.

Example 3

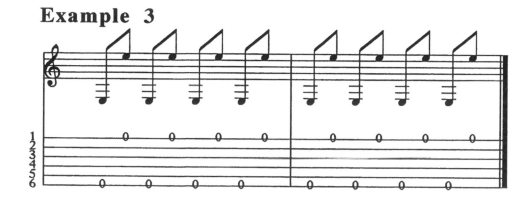

Triplets

Triplets are commonly used in the blues. A triplet is basically three notes per beat, and looks like this:

Example 4

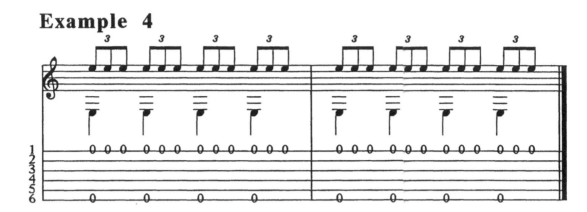

> Practice all three exercises until they feel comfortable. Make sure to get the right hand thumb correct! Make sure it is precisely on the beat, and is very steady. You can mess up the treble and still get away with it, but not the bass. Remember to tap your foot. This will help immensely.

Folk Mote Music, Santa Barbara, CA

Now let's try to play a song using this technique:

Gamblers Blues

Kenny Sultan

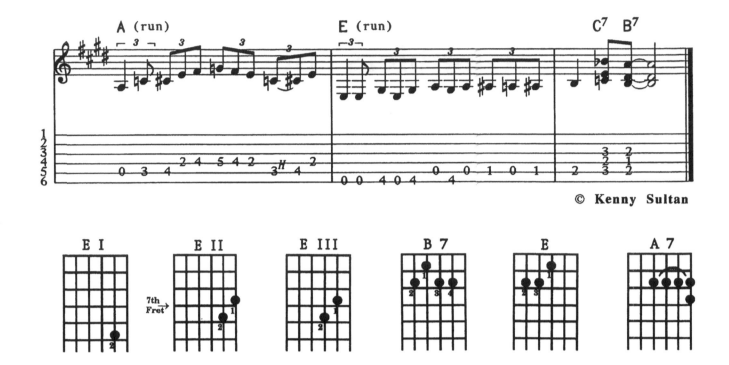

Let's go over what we just played. The first part consists of the same melody note, played in consecutive **triplets**. Hear the difference between the fretted 2nd string and the open 1st string. It is subtle, but it's there. You can slide into the 1st note of the triplet to give it a more bluesy feel (listen to the tape). The **bends** in the 2nd bar are very slight. Do not overbend. The A chord is a series of triplets moving from your 3rd fret, to the 2nd fret, then open on the 1st string, while the 2nd string remains fretted on the 2nd fret in the A position.

In the 7th bar of the song, I use a **brush technique**. Take one finger and brush up on all three strings simultaneously. With this technique it will sound like you are strumming up on the strings. Play this measure forcefully. Remember it's okay to be loose playing the blues as long as the rhythm is steady.

In the 8th and 9th measures, be sure to make the **full chords**. Make a full E chord in the 8th bar and a full B7 chord in the 9th bar. Although you hit only 1 or 2 strings, make the whole chord. By making the complete chord two things are accomplished. The first is that it sharpens up your chord making skills and the second is that if you make a mistake and hit the wrong string, it will still sound good. We end the example with a couple of bass runs. Listen to the tape to hear exactly what they're supposed to sound like. Oh, I almost forgot about the final transition from C7 to B7. To make the C7, I just use a B7 chord and move it up one fret. Maybe I'm lazy, but it's a lot easier than trying to make a C7 and get back to the B7 in time. So make a B7, move it up one fret to C7, and back down to the B7.

This song relies heavily on the brush technique. The first 3 measures are basically
a D7 chord that slides between the 4th, 3rd and 2nd fret. Be sure to pay attention to the left
hand fingering. Good Luck!

Delta Blues

Kenny Sultan

Single String Runs - Hammer Ons

This next song gives you more of a lead guitar feel than the others we have worked with. There are quite a few single string runs along with many hammer ons. Keep the beat steady if possible and be sure to refer to the chord charts.

Unknown Blues

Lonesome Couch Blues should be played a little faster than the other two. This break relies also on single string notes instead of the brush technique used before. The bend on the 10th fret is substantial; try to make it sound as funky as possible. The turnaround is also very tricky. Take your time.

Lonesome Couch Blues

Kenny Sultan

Playing blues in the key of A is very similar to playing blues in the key of E. The three chords we will use are A, D and E7. If you notice, each of these chords has an open string for their respective tonic notes. A, the open 5th string; D, the open 4th string; and E, the open 6th string. Once again, this is very handy when playing acoustic blues. By having open bass notes, it frees your left hand to play more complicated fills.

Let's start out like we did in the key of E, with the blues shuffle rhythm. The blues shuffle in A looks like this:

Shuffle In A

The single string boogie, or the single string shuffle in the key of A looks like this:

Boogie In A

The first song that incorporates lead lines is very similar to Delta Blues in the first chapter. Here we use a D7 chord which you slide up 7 frets to make an A7. Use the 1 finger brush technique... hitting all 3 strings with 1 finger. Play it loose; a little sloppiness is okay.

The Bunk Blues

Kenny Sultan

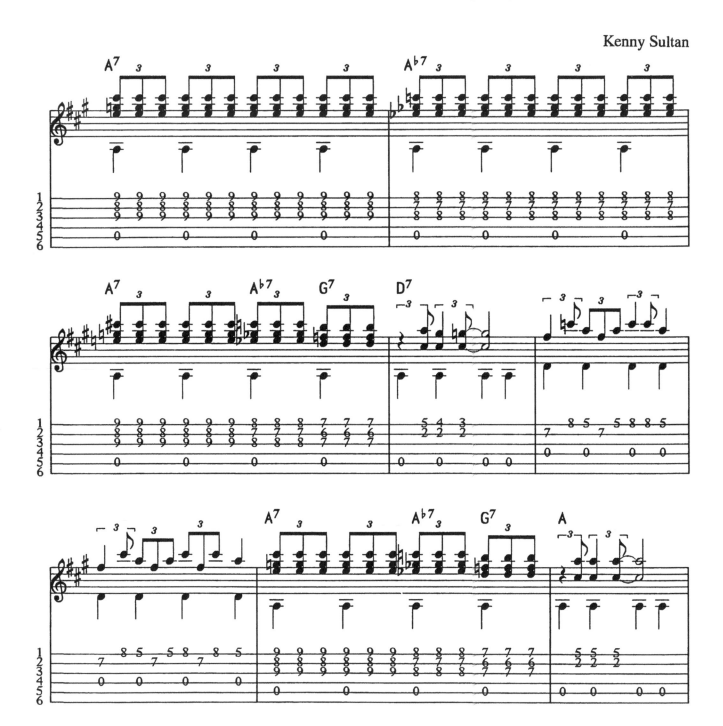

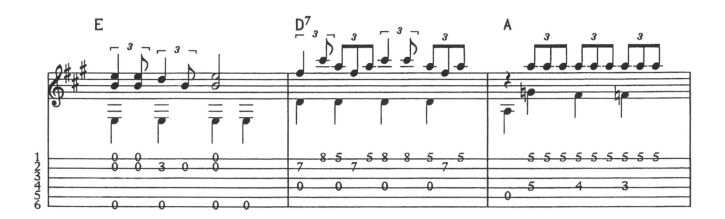

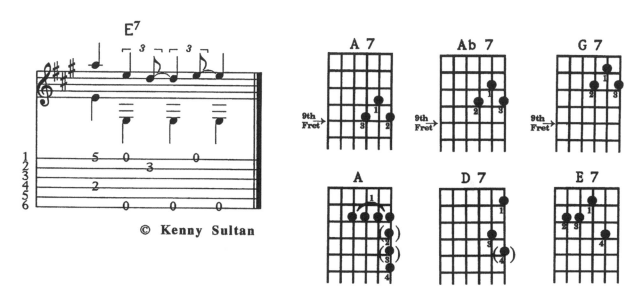

© Kenny Sultan

The first 3 bars should be no trouble. In the 4th bar, be sure to make the full A chord and slide your pinkie down into the A7. The D chord is tricky. Make sure you are fingering it correctly. The rest of the song should be no trouble except for the turnaround, which is quite a stretch, but in time you'll get it.

The N-B Blues

Kenny Sultan

20

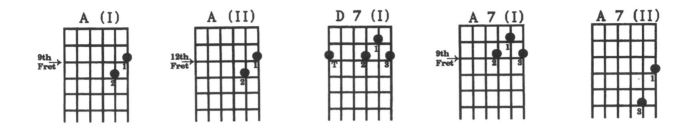

A (I)   A (II)   D 7 (I)   A 7 (I)   A 7 (II)

Let's analyze The N-B Blues. I use my 1st and 2nd finger of my left hand for the 1st four bars, and I slide it from the 9th and 10th fret up to the 12th and 13th fret. The bend occuring at the 12th and 13th fret is small. In bar 5, I use a left hand thumb wrap. I wrap my thumb over the top of the guitar to fret the 2nd fret, 6th string. If you're opposed to wrapping your thumb over the top of the guitar, you can finger it any way you like. It's cool. In the 7th bar, make sure the A7 sustains as long as possible. The rest of the song is not easy, but you should be able to understand it. Just be sure to make the full E chords if possible.

Alternating Bass

To play blues in the key of G, we're going to use an alternating bass instead of the constant bass or monotone bass we've used in the previous chapters. So instead of just hitting the 6th string on the beat, we're going to alternate between the 6th and 4th string. This gives the music a much lighter feel than the more "down home" monotone bass technique. With the alternating bass pattern, the melody falls either directly on the bass note (Example 1), or right in between the bass notes (Example 2). Alternating the chord by lifting the finger off a string and placing it on another string creates different notes.

Blues In G

Example 1

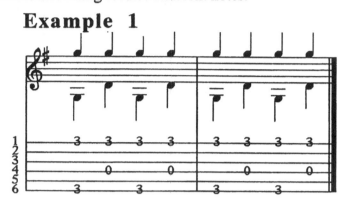

Example 2

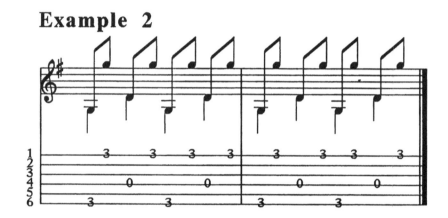

Example 3

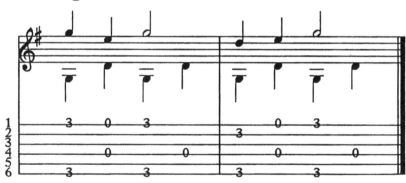

Example 4

Here is an exercise that will hopefully strengthen your right hand and get you used to our new style of playing. Remember, the bass is the most important thing. Make sure it alternates properly and stays on the beat. It will take a lot of practice, so don't get discouraged.

Blues In G

The other chords used in the key of G are C and D or D7. Before we get into some songs, here are some examples of the alternating bass pattern for the C chord and the D chord.

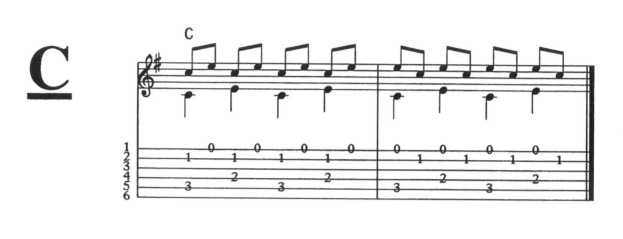

This 12-bar blues form is basically the same as the keys of E and A, except that usually we won't go back to the V chord at the end of each song. Here is your first blues in the key of G.

The song itself is pretty much straight ahead, but your fingers are definately going to get a workout. Be careful of the 2nd half of bar 10. It should basically be played open, except for the 3rd fret, 3rd string. It will take some time to get this song up to speed. Start slowly, and progressively play it faster.

Step It Up And Go

25

Here's an additional break for "Step It Up and Go", or any blues in the key of G. There's a quick G7 in each of the first 4 measures. Be sure to finger the G properly or you won't be able to make the change fast enough. I use my 2nd, 3rd and 4th fingers to make the G chord.

Blues Break "G"

Kenny Sultan

Sometimes you'll want to break up the alternating bass pattern for variety. One way of doing this is playing a boogie. Notice that the treble strings remain the same and the bass notes supply the movement.

Boogie Blues

Kenny Sultan

27

 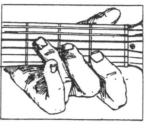 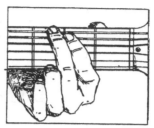

The key of C is one of the most versatile keys. Not only can you play blues, you can play folk, country, ragtime and pop. It's one of my favorite keys. It's a little more difficult than the key of G because of the chords used... most notably the F chord. Some of my favorite players that played almost exclusively in C are Blind Blake, Rev. Gary Davis and Big Bill Broonzy. Since this is a blues book, we will be concentrating only on blues in C. You might notice that these songs have more of a ragtime feel than the keys of E or A. It will be similar to the key of G, but again, different chords, different key, different feel.

WE MAKE THE BLUES SING.

This first example is a straight 12-bar blues, using an alternating bass. Notice the F chord in measure 4. This is best done with the thumb wrapped over the neck on the first fret, 6th string. The bass alternates between the 6th and 4th string. The way I do it is to wrap my thumb over the top and just try to catch some of the string with the excess skin of my thumb. Don't try to wrap it all the way over the top and fret it perfectly. It will put the rest of your fingers out of position. You're likely to get a small buzz out of your 6th string, but this is normal. Try to make this song swing.

Tall Drink Of Water

Kenny Sultan

The next song was made famous by Blind Blake. It was one of the first songs that I learned in the key of C that I could call "authentic blues". I remember when I finally mastered this tune, I knew that this was the style for me. Again, this is basically a 12-bar blues, but notice the quick C to G7 change that takes place throughout the song. If you make a standard G with your first, second or third finger, this is going to be painfully quick. I make my G chord with my third finger, second finger and pinkie. Be sure to refer to the chord examples.

Diddy Wah Diddy

30

The Hesitation Blues is slightly different because, even though it is a "C" blues, it starts off on an A minor chord, the relative minor of C. This is the "Hesitation Blues", made famous by Rev. Gary Davis, and more recently, Hot Tuna.

The Hesitation Blues

Open D - DADF#AD

To play blues in the key of D, we're going to change the tuning of the guitar. We're now going to play in **open D** tuning, also called "Vestapol tuning" or "Cross Note". Down a whole step from open E, its a favorite tuning for many guitarest for its richness and ease of playability. From standard tuning, lower the first, second, and sixth strings one whole step (two frets), and lower the third string one-half step (one fret). Be sure to look at the chord chart to learn the new chords. This is a great tuning, because if you're ever lost, or don't know what you're doing, just strum the guitar open (D chord) and it'll sound good. I've used this trick many times.

Prodigal Son in open D is going to be a finger-picking blues using the same alternating bass principles found in the keys of G and C. There will be some new chord fingerings, so pay close attention. Aside from that, it will be pretty similar to what we've played in the other chapters. Here it is:

Prodigal Son

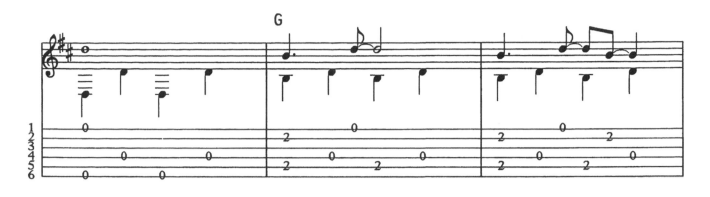

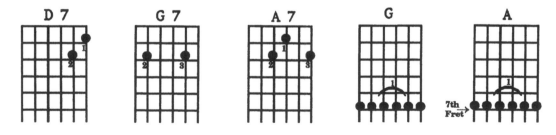

Slides

Slide or Bottleneck

Some of the most exciting blues guitar music has involved the use of a slide, or bottleneck. Robert Johnson, Elmore James, Son House, Ry Cooder and Johnny Winter are some of the players who have used the bottleneck over the years. Most guitar stores offer a variety of manufactured slides in different shapes and sizes. I recommend a heavy, long slide, (glass or metal)... one that will cover all the strings in case you need to make a barre. When you use the slide to fret notes, or to barre, place it directly over the fret wire, not between the frets as you normally would with your fingers. Make sure the slide is straight, in line with the frets, and don't push down too hard on the string. Press lightly. The slide should exert enough pressure to create a tone from the strings, but not so much as to touch the frets or the fingerboard. This will take some practice. Since bottleneck playing is more feel than technique, the accompanying tape will help you out on some of the finer points of playing slide. I also recommend that you place the slide on your pinky so you can still finger chords with your left hand.

Now let's try to add some slide to Prodigal Son. Use the slide to fret all the notes except those located in the last six bars of the song. One way to find out if your intonation is correct is to use your fingers to fret the notes, and then use your slide to make the notes. Try to listen and see if there's any difference in tone. Sometimes the slide will sound flat (you're not moving the slide far enough up the neck) and sometimes the slide will make it sound sharp (you're going too far past the fret wire).

Prodigal Son
With Slide

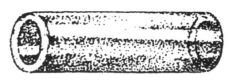

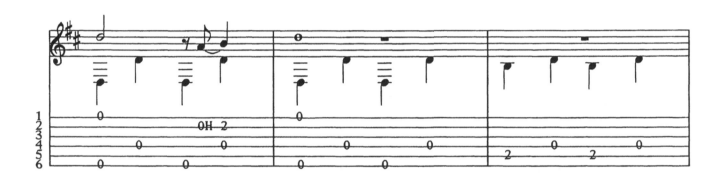

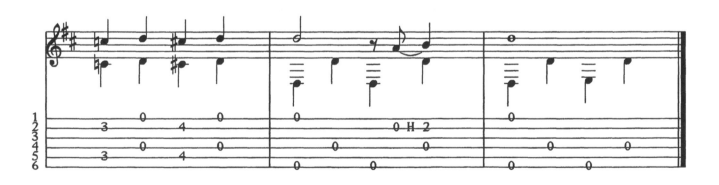

This next example is the "Dust My Broom" lick made famous by Robert Johnson and Elmore James. Do not use the slide in measure eleven or when playing the bass shuffle. Play these notes with the fingers of your left hand.

Dust My Broom

D Tuning - DADF#AD

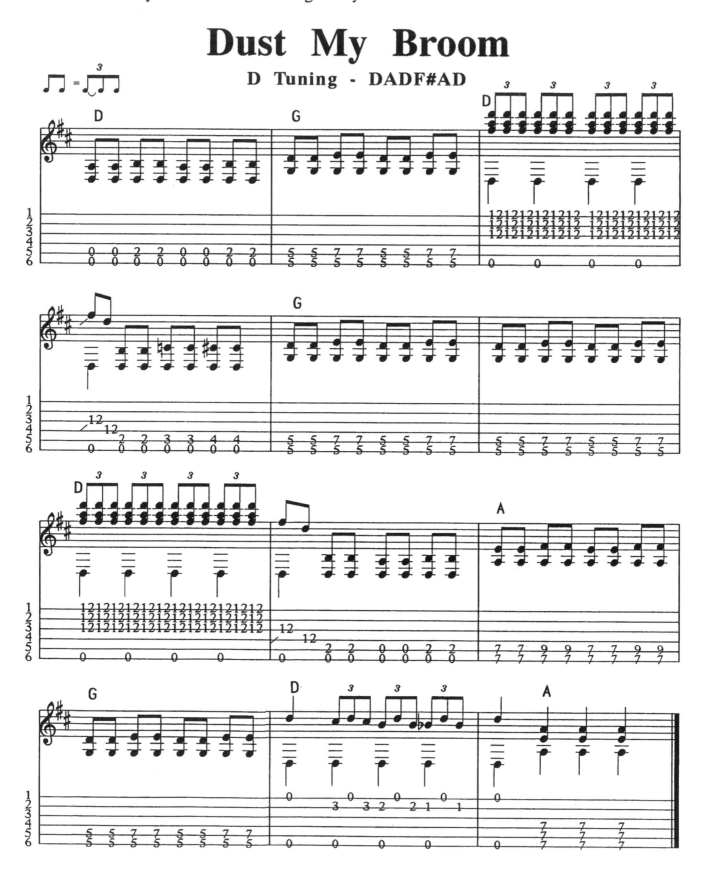

Well, I hope you made it through in one piece. Some of the songs in this book have been known to create major headaches. I figured I would wait until the end to tell you, because that's the kind of guy I am. Just keep plugging away and you'll get it.

Finger Picks - Strings - Capo's

Before we close, there are a few more things I would like to discuss. The first is fingerpicks. I use them, but I'm not sure I would recommend them to students just beginning to play the blues. They are very awkward and hard to get used to. If you want to try anyway, I would recommend a Herco thumbpick, and Dunlop fingerpicks. The picks will make your guitar sound louder, enable you to play faster and make the brush technique easier. But again, they are difficult to use.

Thumb Picks

Finger Picks

Capo's

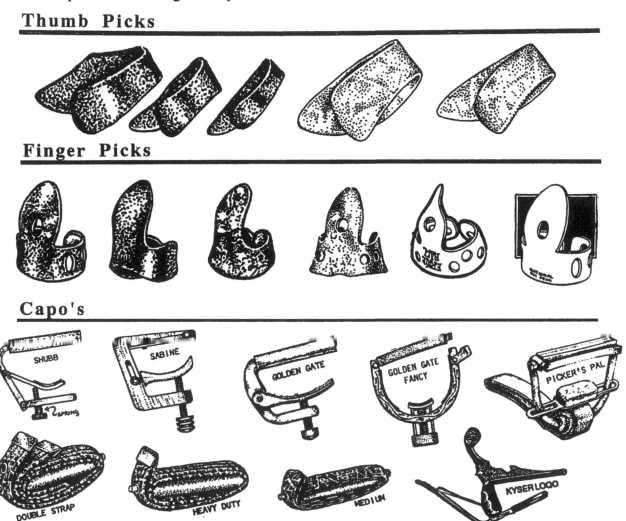

My favorite strings are made by John Pearse. If these aren't available, Martin guitar strings are excellent. I use medium gauge, but I suggest you use light gauge until your callouses build up. As far as a capo, there is only one that works for me, and it is made by Schubb. It is easy to get on and off the guitar neck, and doesn't pull the strings out of tune.

The guitars I play vary, but my two favorites are a 1936 Martin 00018, and a new Santa Cruz OM model. Both guitars are terrific for blues and fingerstyle guitar, and I recommend both models highly.

It is very important to listen to as much blues as possible when learning this style. The musicians I think you should listen to include Blind Blake, Blind Boy Fuller, Rev. Gary Davis, John Hammond, Ry Cooder, David Bromberg, Lightnin' Hopkins, Robert Johnson, Taj Mahal and Brownie McGhee. Try to find the records where they play solo, or records that use as little accompaniment as possible. This way you'll be able to hear the guitar better. I personally have four albums out, with my partner **Tom Ball.** Tom is an excellent harmonica player/vocalist/guitarist, but he could use some brushing up on his poker playing skills! I've been working with him for the last 10 years, and we cover a variety of blues and ragtime styles. These albums are available from your better record stores, or through Flying Fish Records, 1304 West Shubert, Chicago, IL 60614 or from myself, Kenny Sultan, PO Box 20156, Santa Barbara, CA 93120.

Tom Ball & Kenny Sultan

Also feel free to write me if you have any questions about the book. I'm happy to say that this is just the first in a series of blues guitar books that I will be doing for Ron Middlebrook at Centerstream Publications. So keep an eye out for Blues Guitar #2. Until then, good luck with your playing, and when it doubt...**wing it.**

More Great Guitar Books from Centerstream...

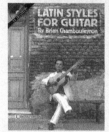

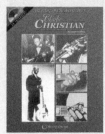
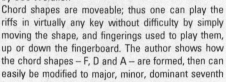